EVERNOTE

Discover The Life Changing Power of Evernote

Quick Start Guide To Improve Your Productivity And Get Things Done At Lightning Speed!

By: Matthew Barton

Table of Content

Introduction

I want to thank you and congratulate you for purchasing the book, *"Evernote: Discover The Life Changing Power of Evernote. Quick Start Guide To Improve Your Productivity And Get Things Done At Lightning Speed!* This book has everything you need to know to transform your life by unleashing the full power of Evernote.

We all have many things to do. This means that we somehow need to have a way of remembering everything that needs to be done. In a typical scenario, the conventional notebook or a diary does the trick just fine. But it has its downsides one of them being that you cannot always carry around your diary or notebook. This coupled with the tediousness of carrying notebooks around and the fact that you are limited on what you can capture makes the conventional notebook or diary a not so good of an option. That's not all; you probably will find yourself having a hard time rummaging through the tons of notebooks or diaries that you've accumulated over the years just to find some important information that you captured. This can be pretty overwhelming at times.

Well, fortunately, you now don't have to go through all that trouble in trying to capture ideas, to dos, etc thanks to Evernote. If you sometimes feel overwhelmed by the overload of information that you want to capture or retrieve, Evernote is your best bet to turn around the situation.

Over the last five years, Evernote has created a name for itself as one of the most powerful productivity tools used by thousands of professional around the world. In Evernote, there are no limitations. What you get is limited only by your own imagination. Evernote is designed for modern day on-the-go idea capture, note taking, and writing. From project plans to meeting notes, everything you write in Evernote stays with you everywhere you go. For project collaboration, you can work with your teams without minding if the teams/colleagues are across the room or on the other side of the globe.

Evernote also makes knowledge sharing and project collaboration easier and more effective by making it easy to gather research by way of clipping and saving articles with the Web Clipper tool built into Evernote. Further, Evernote allows you to collect all physical and digital details for your projects in one place. This combined with the easy-to-use, but powerful search feature, makes finding documents, text, and images anytime, anywhere, and across all of your devices lightning fast.

Do you want to stay organized and productive as you work towards completing your projects and achieving your goals? Use Evernote. Don't know how to get started? You're in luck because Evernote and how you can use it to stay organized and productive is our focus. You will discover some Evernote secrets that will supercharge your productivity.

Thanks again for purchasing this book, I hope you enjoy it!

information is without contract or any type of guarantee assurance.

The trademarks that are used are without any consent, and the publication of the trademark is without permission or backing by the trademark owner. All trademarks and brands within this book are for clarifying purposes only and are the owned by the owners themselves, not affiliated with this document.

Section 1: Getting Started With Evernote

What is Evernote?

Evernote is a "freemium", cross- platform app designed for note taking, organizing, and archiving. The app allows users to create notes in any form such as; formatted text, webpage, or webpage excerpt, photographs, screenshots, voice memos or a handwritten note. Notes created in Evernote can be sorted into folders, annotated, tagged, edited, and exported as a part of notebook.

As you can note, you can really consider Evernote to be a digital notebook, which you can use to capture inspiration, work notes, To-do lists, and just about anything else you can think of. Part of the reason why Evernote is so compelling is because of its extensive cross-platform support; it is available for Mac OS X, Windows, Android, Blackberry, Windows phone, and Evernote web browser.

So how can you really benefit from using Evernote? Let's look at some of its benefits:

Benefits of Using Evernote

If you're wondering if using Evernote is a sound decision, here are some known benefits of using the platform in your everyday life.

1. *Note Content Types*

Most Evernote users think of text notes whenever they think

of Evernote. In addition to being great at storing text notes, the app can maintain a wide range of content. For example, you can store images with text included, you can upload an image directly from your computer or take one with your phone device, upload a PDF file, capture screenshots, store links, and archives of various websites and even record audio notes. Obviously, a conventional notebook or diary cannot have all these features.

2. Optical Character Recognition (OCR)

Once you upload an image into Evernote, the application immediately scans it for readable text. If it finds any, it makes that text searchable. For example, if you scan a dinner receipt, even if you don't save or remember the name of the restaurant in the note, you can search the restaurant by its name and find your receipt.

Note: If you have a premium account, Evernote will use OCR to help you search content contained in PDF files.

3. Cloud Management

All Evernote content stays online by default. This keeps away the hustle of manually synchronizing local copies into your devices. For native clients, you can set your data to a local storage. However, Evernote tries to sync the notes every 5, 10, 15 or 30 minutes depending on how you set it, which simply means that you can access your notes from any device. Additionally, the fact that it stores local copies in each of the connected devices means that you can work on your notes even if you don't have internet connection. And even if you uninstall the app from one device, you can still access the notes using the web app or after installing another copy in another device. Everything is stored in cloud.

Note: Evernote premium users can access their notes history to restore information from older versions of a note. In addition, if you use Evernote business, you can easily manage your project and co-workers work-data without keeping track of multiple files, programs and emails.

4. Multi-Platform Support

If you have an internet-connected device, you can store content in Evernote through the web app. Additionally, not only does Evernote offer native clients for IOS, Android, blackberry and windows phones, it also has clients for windows and OS X.

Moreover, on top of using mobile devices and native clients to manage content in Evernote, you can also use tools such as the Penultimate and browser add-ons such as the Evernote web clipper to add and manage content to Evernote from any device. When you are on a public computer, you can add notes to Evernote through email or log in through the browser.

5. Tagging and Organization

Evernote has a sophisticated organization system that not only allows you to categorize notes into various notebooks, but also allows you a chance to bunch multiple notebooks together into a mass notebook. In addition, you can tag all your notes for easy review later. Your notes can have multiple tags that will allow you to easily search for data. If you prefer, you can create shortcuts that help you rapidly select frequently accessed data and sort the results in searches for better results.

Did you know that Evernote has the potential to change your life? Yes, it can! While Evernote seems like a simple application, it has a massive impact on your day-to-day life in terms of productivity and organization.

The following are some suggestions on how the use of Evernote can improve your productivity.

Can Evernote Change Your Life and Productivity?

The answer is yes. Here are a few reasons why:

✓ With Evernote, you can copy email threads containing important information, or are worthy of keeping straight into a new note.

✓ Evernote changes your traditional means of taking notes while in meetings. Instead of using paper and pen to write down agendas, you can use Evernote's audio record feature to record a meeting. After the meeting, you can listen to your audio as you type in notes in the same folder housing the audio. This gives you the chance to recap the meeting and clarify or expand your notes.

✓ Evernote is ideal for those inspirational moments that seem to strike when you least expect it. With the platform, you can easily save your impromptu ideas. This is especially useful when an idea seems fleeting and you're afraid you might lose your train of thought. In this instance, all you have to do is start a new note and use the audio recorder to speak out your thoughts.

✓ Evernote is your filing cabinet. Evernote can organize all your receipts, paperwork and keep you organized and productive. Instead of using a normal filing system to house your documents, you can scan them, save them in Evernote, and store the original away in the attic. Note tags make it easy to review notes whenever you want after creating them. The platform also makes it possible to access all your files from your phone or any other internet-connected device.

✓ Evernote makes task management and tracking easy: Evernote allows you to create tick/check boxes for items you need to follow up. When done, tick, and that's all. Any notes or history you have about those particular items will be kept alongside the to-do list item, including your files, photos, or audio.

Evernote is a productivity app; it helps you to note down your to dos, ideas, thoughts, memories etc with lightning speed so that you can focus on important things instead of having to think about them regularly just to make sure you don't forget. All this boils down to one thing and this is getting things done. So how does Evernote help you to get things done? We will learn all that in the next chapter.

Evernote's GTD Principle

GTD or 'getting things done' is a 'staying-productive-and-getting-organized-system'. The GTD method is used to organize your to-do list, your schedule and your priorities in a manageable manner.

Learning the different GTD principles can help you to easily glimpse what you have on your device (Evernote account) and choose what to work on next. Moreover, it places strong emphasis on shifting your to-do's from your head into an easy to reference system. This clears your overall mind of any mental distractions that may keep you from working effectively and being productive.

Unfortunately, GTD has a reputation for being complicated. This is because there is no "right" way to practice it. Nevertheless, here are a few tips to help you get things done through Evernote:

1. Capture Everything

Capture your ideas, you to-dos, your recurring task, etc. Type them into an Evernote notebook. Note that the greatest barrier to effectively using GTD principal with Evernote is the notion of "I will add the items to my list later". You need to capture everything when it happens and avoid thinking about it until it's time to complete it. It is the only way you can de-clutter your mind to maintain the much-needed focus.

2. Clarify the Things You Have To Do

Writing down tasks and to-dos is not enough. Create time to break down the tasks and goals into actionable steps to avoid any barrier of doing the task. If there's anything you can do right away, do it. Anything you can delegate, delegate it. You can have different notebooks, with proper tagging, which clearly outline what it is you should do and what is to be done by someone else. In so doing, you can be sure of having undivided focus.

3. Organize

Organize your actionable items by priority and category. While doing this, assign their due dates where necessary, and set reminders you can follow up on. Try to pay special attention to each item's priority. This does not mean you are working on your items right now; you are just making sure they are on their right position in the completion order priority. All this can be done through Evernote i.e. setting reminders, categorizing notes into their respective notebooks, tagging and naming of titles.

4. Reflect On Your To-Do List

Your first step should be looking over your to-do list and determining what your next action should be. You should be able to pick the item from your list and have the energy and time to do it right away. In case you find an item you can't work on at the spot, break it down.

Next, give your to-do list a periodically in-depth review to see where you're making progress, where adjustment of your priorities is required and verify how the system is working for you.

5. Engage and Get To Work

It's time to choose your next action and start working on it. Your to dos are organized by priority and placed by categories. This means you know what to work on and when.

Section 2: Evernote How Tos

On a previous chapter, we referred to Evernote as a note-taking platform, an archiving platform, and an organization tool. However, none of these terms are enough to completely convey how much you can do with this amazing platform.

The tools associated with Evernote are utterly great. There are plenty of methods and practices for getting the most out of the Evernote service. This starts from what you can store; addresses, recipes, travel info, business cards, projects notes, entire articles and just everything, to how you can store these notes in Evernote, and to what you can do with the data after.

Below are crucial tips you need to know to get the most out of Evernote. If you use the platform correctly, it will become an invaluable productivity and organizational tool.

How To Create New Notes, Organize Notebooks And Share Your Notes In Evernote

Evernote is a modern, digital workspace that enables you to increase your productive by giving you access to a note-taking platform usable across multiple digital platforms. To start using Evernote, you need to learn how to create, organize, and share notes.

While the prospect of taking notes seems foreign and outdated, it is the first step to using this very powerful platform. Here is a breakdown of the powerful features provided by notes in Evernote.

Taking notes-you can do this by writing down information from short lists to lengthy research notes

Collecting everything-you can save content from multiple sources to one place. This can be handwritten notes, screenshots, audio files, web articles, and pictures.

Finding what you need-you can easily search all your saved notes and access information you need for your project

Sharing your work- You can share with others what you are working on to collaborate better with them.

Creating a New Note in Evernote

Note: The images here are created from Evernote's IOS version. Please note that your PC might have a different layout but the functioning is fairly similar.

Follow the simple steps below to create a new text note:

Step 1: click on the (+) sign from the side of the navigation menu to create a new blank page.

Step 2: start by giving your note a title by simply keying in the note title on the section labeled "title your note".

Step 3: click on the next text field and then type your text and input data into your note to create a text note.

How to create note for IOS

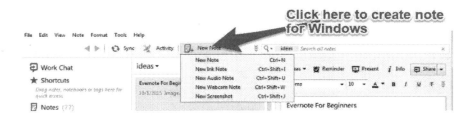

These are not the only ways through which you can create notes on Evernote across different platforms. On Windows for instance, you can follow the following approaches:

✓ File>>New Note

✓ Ctrl + N

✓ Right click on a note (from the "all notes list") then click new note

Organizing Notebooks In Evernote

To move your notes into various notebooks, follow these simple 2 steps

Step 1: select the note you intend to move, and click on the name of the current notebook located on top of the note title. You will see a dropdown menu with a list of all the existing notebooks.

Step 2: select the field where you want to save your notebook. In most cases, new notes are automatically saved to the default notebook that comes with your account.

The image below shows how to do that with an IOS version of Evernote.

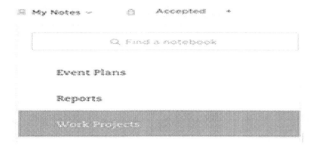

The image below shows how to do that using Windows desktop client.

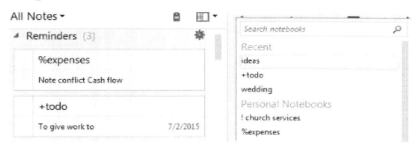

Note: The above two are not the only ways you can organize notes. For instance, you can simply right click on the note (from the "all notes list"), then choose "move to notebook" or "copy to notebook".

Keeping your Evernote notes and files organized is key to staying organized and productive. Often, your organization in Evernote will vary from user to user depending on how each user defines his or her organizational structure.

In terms of organization, there are some standard global labels that you can employ to organize your Evernote notes; below are just a few of these note labels.

!Inbox notebook (the default notebook) - Any note that does not go into a content specific folder goes into the default folder. Create this folder because it will appear at the top of your notebooks and serve to remind you the importance of organizing your notes accordingly.

!Action Notebook- The action notebook serves as a reminder of time sensitive tasks begging for completion within a specific timeline. By using the "!" we ensure that the notebook appears amongst the top notebooks and thus grabs our attention. Use this notebook to store notes that require immediate attention within 72Hrs.

!Ideas Notebook-the Ideas notebook is a spur of the moment notebook.

!Random Notebook-Often times, you will experience random thoughts you can turn into flourishing ideas. Store these in your random notebook. By labeling notes as random, you can revisit them later, develop them, and move them into an appropriate notebook.

Strive to develop and nurture the habit of using tags as often as you can because they help create an easier way of file retrieval. The above organizational structure is much better than letting all your notes go into one cluttered Default Notebook. Part of the reason I recommend this structure is that letting your default notebook get cluttered means you will have to work extra hard and allocate time to perform some proper organization. Develop this structure and habit earlier on and you are off to a good start in your organizational goals.

Sharing Notes with Others

To share your Evernote notes, simply follow these steps:

Step 1: select a note from your list of notes, click on the share icon at the top right side of the screen

Step 2: select at least one recipient, type a message concerning the note if necessary then click on the send icon.

Note: The first image below is for IOS while the other is for Windows desktop client.

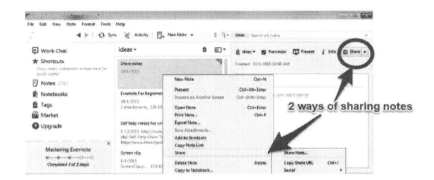

Using Evernote To Create A Table Of Content With Note Links

Note links allow you to link together different notes and help you create a customized and organized structure inside your Evernote account. Note links are great for linking up various pieces of travel related information's such as articles, itineraries, and passport photos, including organizing projects tools and class research.

One crucial thing you can do with note links is creating a table of content for a set of notes in a notebook. This is useful particularly when you intend to share your notebook. Below are steps you can follow to create a table of content with note links.

Step #1: Capture a note link by right clicking on the note and selecting the "copy note link" option

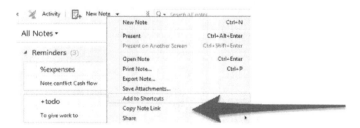

Step #2: In your notebook, create a new note or go to the note you would want that note link to go

Step #3: paste the link on the new note. It will appear as a hyperlinked title of your note into your new note or on the existing note.

Step #4: repeat the procedure for all other notes you would like to include in your table of contents; put them in the order that you would like other people to view them on the notebook.

How to Manage Note and Tasks in Evernote

Even though Evernote makes it easy to search for content, it is best practice to establish a way of managing and naming your notes and tasks for easier and faster search and archiving.

To manage your notes, follow these 3 tips:

Tip#1: Create a Logical Notebook Structure

You can manage your notebooks in various ways. For instance, you can manage them by department or group, project title or status or by customer accounts.

Example

Product development

Project x: Comprised of designs, specs, meeting notes and tasks

Human resources

New employees hand book: contains different views discussed by the entire company; benefits, company holidays, policies, charts, and procedures

Tip#2: Define a Set of Reusable Tags

Add some searchable tags referring to a project, company, project status, project or task owner or any other term that is easier to filter out of the content.

Example

Type	*tag used*
Location:	recruiting: New York, Miami, Mexico
Status/phase	task management: next, now completed

Tip#3: Establish Naming Conventions

Naming conventions make it effortless for everyone in the company to manage and find content rapidly. For instance, you can come up with a set of guideline that every department or group should use a specific code. This code will be used to search all their notebooks in the devices. i.e.: MKTG for marketing

Evernote provides a central spot for monitoring and managing all your tasks. Below are simple ways you can use to manage your tasks.

#1: Create one note to rule them all. To get started with managing your tasks, create a new note. You can add and modify your tasks from a note no matter where you access Evernote.

#2: Return to check: in your note, add a check box and add your first task in it. Once you click "return" automatically, you will create another checkbox for the next task. While on the go, manage your task by clicking on the check box on your tablet, phone, or watch

#3: Checklist in a flash: Using Mac's Evernote platform, you can take your list of items and transform it to checklist immediately.

#4: Be bold: To balance various categories of tasks on your notebook, separate them with bolded titles and choose different color and fonts

#5: Link to tasks: If most of your tasks relate to certain work you have worked on in Evernote, connect them with note links

#6: Take shortcuts: Spend less time trying to find your to-do lists by creating shortcuts. Learn how to create a shortcut on devices like Mac, IOS, Windows, and Android.

How To Plan And Effectively Use Tags To Increase Productivity

Tags are attributes applied to any individual note. By specifying tags, you can review all notes under that tag regardless of where a particular note resides. You can organize your notes using the following three categories of tags:

Descriptors: you can add tag referring to the source of notes, conversations, and media types.

Knowledge: Based on the kind of information contained within a note

Projects: These tags are placed in notes associated with a specific type of work you are actively completing.

Note that tags should appear alphabetically. Use symbols such as periods, hash tags, and numbers that force them into a sequence that works for you.

How to add tags in Evernote

Evernote users can create as many tags as they need. This means that all your notes can be associated with multiple tags.

Below is how to add a tag to your notes:

Step 1: open the note you intend to tag

Step 2: open the tags editor

Step 3: type any word or phrase you want to use as a tag. As you type, tag suggestions from previous tags used in Evernote will appear.

Step 4: Once you settle on a tag for your note, add the tag to the note by pressing return (enter)

Step 5: If you want to delete a tag, backspace over the tag text.

You can still add tags by platform:

Windows or Mac desktop: at the top of your note, on the right side of the notebook name, click to add tags and follow the previous procedure

IPhone, iPad, and iPod touch: below the note title, click the "i" icon and tap on the add tag icon. Follow the procedure above.

Web browser: on the right side of your note, select info and click on (+) tags.

How To Forward And Organize Emails In Evernote

Once you sign up for a free or premium Evernote account, Evernote assigns you a free email account specific to that Evernote account. In the info of your account, you should see an email address listed as follows "email notes to". That is your Evernote email address:

Evernote gives you 3 simple tips to organize your important emails categorizing them by note, notebook and tags.

Forwarding an Email Directly To a Specific Notebook on Evernote

At the end of your subject line, add the symbol @ together with the name of the notebook you intend to forward your email to. Ensure to correctly type the name exactly as it appears on your Evernote account including the spaces in between the words. Below is an illustration.

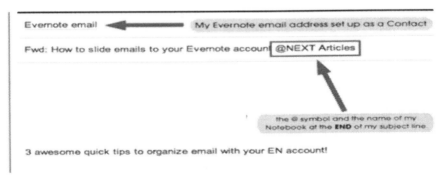

Tip #2: Including Tags in Your Email

At the end of the subject line, incorporate the # symbol together with any other tags you would like to add to that email. Ensure that you have an existing tags system for your Evernote account.

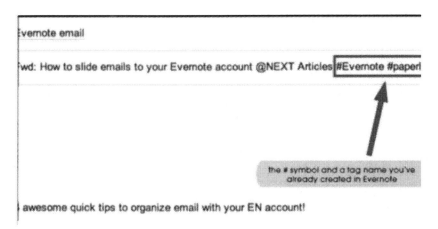

Tip #3: Sending Your Emails to Evernote

By hitting send, you will have organized the email into your Evernote notebook

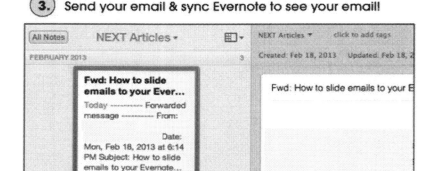

Now that you have learnt how to organize your email, let us look at steps you can use to forward email to Evernote

Step 1: Locate your Evernote's Emails Address

The first step is to look for your email address inside your account info or settings. On most devices, you will find the email address by clicking on the username icon and navigating to account info. Below are the specific instructions you can use to find your email address for various platforms and devices.

Evernote for windows: on the device, click on the tools icon, and then account info. Your email address should appear next to an email notes to...(as shown below).

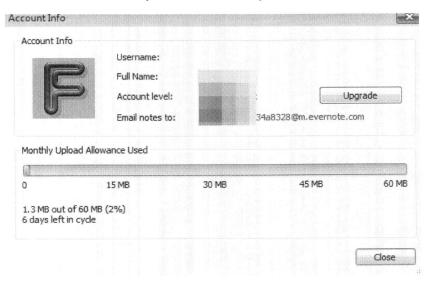

Evernote for Mac: Click on your username and select the account info. Your email will be shown below the email notes to icon.

Evernote for iPad, iPhone and iPod touch: tap your username

to access your account settings. Scroll down the list and select the "general" icon, then click on Evernote email address.

Evernote for Android: click on the Evernote menu, select the settings icon, scroll down until you see your Evernote account email address.

Step 2: Forwarding an Email Into The Evernote

When forwarding an email into the Evernote account, enter your Evernote email address in the recipient filed. Automatically, your subject will become the title to your new note. After sending the email message, it will appear as a note on your Evernote account.

How To Scan Documents Into Evernote

Scanning documents into Evernote is a great way to bridge your physical and digital world. You probably have all kind of papers and receipts scattered everywhere. Evernote can help you go paperless. Here is how.

Step 1: Buy An Evernote-Compatible Scanner: There are many Evernote compatible scanners. For example, printer models like, canon, Fujitsu, scan snap, Lexmark, and s1300 are all highly compatible with Evernote. An Evernote compatible scanner will save you from scanning files into PDF then exporting the document into Evernote.

Step 2: Set Up the Scanner: To set up the scanner, set up an Evernote profile manually; this can be done by downloading the scan snap manager software. Once it is set up, just insert your paper document, and push a button to start scanning.

Step3: Gather All Documents You Would like to Scan: There is nothing you can't scan into your Evernote account. Gather all your bills, receipts, manuals and any other piece of paper you need to scan into Evernote. Scan snap can handle all sizes of paper up to 9 inches wide papers. You can scan any form of paper as long as it's not thicker than a normal paper.

Step 4: Start Scanning: After inserting the documents you are scanning in the scanner, press the scan button. This will take you a few minutes after which, you will notice that the scanned images will be a bit perfectly vertical compared to the real documents.

Step 5: File And Tag Each Item: enter "metadata" information for all your Evernote scans, i.e. information concerning that particular image. For instance, for receipts, start with the date, vendor and amount. Ensure to use minimal tags for each item to make finding items faster and easier.

How To Automate Productivity Using Evernote And IFTTT

IFTT (if this then that) is a free web service enabling you to connect two web applications for automated tasks operation. This makes it easy to automate different processes thus freeing your time and making your task performance efficient. To help you understand this better, let's look at a few ways in which you to make this possible:

5 Ways To Use IFTT and Evernote

There are many ways to automate productivity with IFTTT and Evernote. Here are five great ways that will help you to automate your productivity:

#1: **Create a note from your calendar events**

You can easily use the IFTTT task "recipe" to create a new note in your chosen notebook for a new calendar event on your Google calendar 15 minutes before the start time of a meeting.

This is a great way of saving time since you can start a note for an upcoming meeting with pre-populated information. Since you type the note in Evernote, after the meeting ends, you can easily share it with your team members. You can check out the IFTTT recipe on how to do this.

#2: **Connecting Your Android Phone and Evernote**

IFTTT has a phone number you can send your text messages and voice notes to. For example, to write down your thought before it slips away, rather than opening your Evernote account or draft, you can easily send a text message to IFTTT with a certain specific hashtag, and the note will automatically go to the right Evernote notebook.

On the other hand, by calling your IFTTT number, it instantly records your voice message and moves it to the right Evernote notebook. This a great option for capturing vital information and shifting it in Evernote. Here is the IFTTT recipe for that.

#3: Centralizing Crucial Emails within Evernote

Assuming you have an Evernote notebook you use to store your online purchase receipts, you can easily automate this process by you having every email you receive from Apple, Google, iTunes, Amazon, etc. sent to a specific Evernote notebook and tag. Check out the recipe for saving your receipts here.

Plus, using another IFTTT task, any "starred' emails in Gmail will create a new note automatically in a designated Evernote notebook and tag

#4: Saving Your Favorite Tweets and Articles to Evernote

As mentioned earlier, you can capture and collect important information you will need later for specific projects or for general reference with IFTTT. IFTTT allows you to easily read articles from pocket or instapaper, and forward send your favorite tweets to Evernote, or add pictures to Evernote each time you're tagged in a photo on Facebook. Here is the IFTTT recipe for saving your favorite tweets.

#5: Sending RSS Feeds To Evernote

If you're a fan of RSS feeds as a way of staying updated you don't have to read them directly from Google. Leverage IFTTT for Evernote. You can do this by copying the RSS URL that interest you and add it to IFTTT. The RSS feed will forward to a specific tag and Evernote notebook you designate.

Note: When you combine IFTTT with Evernote, the result is truly something beyond powerful. You can check out the IFTTT recipes that you can use to really make some of the redundant time consuming activities easy to undertake since they will be all automated.

Evernote Search Commands Guaranteed To Rocket Fuel Your Productivity

Evernote can organize your life and keep you on the path to being efficient. Moreover, the Evernote platform can be omnipresent, and you can use it for your personal, professional, or important day-to-day note taking and idea capture.

After long continuous use of the platform, you will have to perform more searches while searching your Evernote for notes/ideas you need to work on. Normally, most Evernote users use a keyword to search note. The resulting results are a large number of results especially if you have a lot of information with similar topics.

Fortunately, Evernote search system has offered an advanced syntax that gives you a precise way of searching your notes. The following is a quick guide:

- ✓ While searching for tag within your existing tags, type *tag:thetagname, or tag:multiple-wordthetagname* into the search field.

- ✓ While searching for notes within notebooks with specific terms in their names, type *notebook:yournotebookname / notebook: "multiple-word yournotebookname"* in the search field

- ✓ To search for notes containing a specific keyword inside, type *any:keyword1 keyword2 keyword3* in the search field.

✓ You can also search based on creation date, and content by using an 8 digits number to signify the date, such as *created:yyyymmdd*

✓ When you want to get results based on the last time a certain note was revised, type *updated:yyyymmdd* on the Evernote's search field.

✓ While searching for a note containing a specific term in its title, type *intitle:term* or *intitle: "multiple –word term"*

Section3: Evernote Tips And Tricks: Using Evernote To Organize Your Life

Evernote, being a useful platform enabling you to organize and collect your notes, has many other uses you might not have known before. Besides jotting down your thoughts, maintaining your to-do list and saving your web pages, below are some of tricks and tips you can use to maximize your productivity:

Use Evernote to Set Reminders

Did you know you could set a reminder on your android phone or desktop using the Evernote app? You can do this by clicking on the alarm clock icon on top of any saved note.

After setting a reminder, you will get an in-app alarm and an email on the date you have set the reminder.

Enable 2-Step Verification to Keep Your Evernote Secure

While setting 2-step verification, you will need to enter a randomly generated verification code in addition to your password and username the first time you log in to your account from any device you use including your computer.

Your verification codes will be sent to you via text message or within you code generation app created by Evernote on your phone.

To activate this feature, go to Evernote settings on the web and select security.

Note that this feature is available only to Evernote premium users or business accounts.

Use Evernote with Other Apps

You can start using Evernote along with other favorite apps. For instance, if you're a fan of RSS readers, you can freely sync your Evernote account to automatically save articles from RSS to your notebook at the click of a button.

Evernote web clipper

You can use the Evernote web clipper to save web pages quickly on the go. The web clipper is available for modern browsers. It's an easy way to clip a certain web page for later referencing or reading.

Evernote web clipper is now available for Firefox, Google chrome, opera, safari and internet explorer.

Store Your Hard Copies as Soft Copies

You can take photos of business cards and meeting white boards and save them in your Evernote notebook. This makes the content searchable just like any other note. You can create a Digital copy of any physical item you have whether it is a hand written note or documents.

Share Your Shopping List with Friends/ Family Members via Evernote

Are you planning to get a roommate? You can now set up a shared list to identify what each of you has. Simply drop a note that has a checklist into your notebook, and share it with someone. If you're a premium user, you can allow the person you have shared your note with to edit the list.

Email Yourself Notes via Evernote

You can email yourself a note and it will be automatically added to your notebook. Every Evernote user has a unique email address, and you can use yours to send yourself notes especially when you are in hurry. We've already discussed how to do this.

Use Evernote Skitch to Annotate Notes, Documents and Photos

Skitch is a separate app owned by Evernote. It is a great app you can use to draw on your documents and photos while pointing out something crucial. This comes in handy if you want to make some illustrations on images for easier understanding.

Skitch is freely available for iOS and android.

Link Notes to Keep Relevant Information Together

Select the note link you intend to link to a note, right click on the note, and then select to copy the note link. Paste the link and it will appear as a hyperlinked title on your note. We've already discussed this.

Evernote Food App

Are you a fan of food photography? Evernote defines its food app as a tool to inspire your food life. It is a great way to explore recipes from sites around the web. You can choose to share the meals with friends and find nearby restaurants.

The Evernote food is free and available for android and iOS.

Note: Evernote has discontinued support for its Food app.

Upgrade to Evernote Premium If You Are a Power User

Evernote premium is a paid service (normally paid $5 per month and $45 per year). A premium user can access notebooks while offline, allow the editing of shared notes, add a pass code lock to the device, upload content up to 1 GB capacity, and search and attach PDFs documents faster than a normal Evernote user. You also get to access some advanced power user features that you don't get access to as a free user.

Connect Pocket and Evernote

With pocket, you can easily grab images, links, and videos and save them for later review. Pocket also eliminates the clutter from articles and saves them in an easy to read way and format. Most applications integrate with pocket, for easy reading and sending of articles and other items send an item from pocket to Evernote.

Use Augment When In Desktop

Augment is a nifty chrome plugin that allows you to manage multiple apps from Gmail. It synchronizes flawlessly with Evernote meaning you easily push a complete email from Gmail to a notebook of your choice or make notes from Gmail without switching your tabs. With the plugin, you will not have to first send the email to a notebook by forwarding it to your Evernote personal email address. Get the plugin here.

Use IFTTT to Send Newsletters to Automatically Evernote

You probably get many informational and promotional newsletters. You can use IFTTT to automatically send all your newsletters to your notebook for future reference.

Stack Notes

We tend to make multiple notes while working on something. Evernote can simplify the task by stacking multiple notes. This feature works on both mobile apps and desktops. Simply select the notes you intend to merge and tap on "merge" icon.

Use Audio and Ink Notes

You can easily click on a photo of your handwriting and save it directly into Evernote. This feature applies to tablets and android phones.

Audio notes are helpful during meetings, speeches, and lectures. They act just like regular notes with tags and are classified into notebooks.

Using Tags and Notebooks

You can organize your notes structure by using tags and notebooks. You can achieve this by forming a reusable and helpful tag defining a context. However, Evernote supports three types of tags: business, personal and shared. Under each of these categories, you can create multiple tags. Notebooks and tags are helpful when you are searching for your data.

Conclusion

Thank you again for purchasing this book!

I hope this book was able to help you to understand how to unleash the full power of Evernote to transform your life.

The next step is to implement what you've learnt to supercharge your productivity, organize your life and get rid of clutter in your life.

Finally, if you enjoyed this book, would you be kind enough to leave a review for this book on Amazon?

Thank you and good luck!

Your Bonus Gift!

Just incase you missed my offer. To show my appreciate to everyone for purchasing this
book. I'm giving away a **BONUS GIFT** exclusive to readers of my book

Would you like to make money while you sleep

Have you ever dreamt or imagined that's its possible to make money even when you are relaxed & fast asleep in your bed? Well it's true! And, we can help you make those dreams or thoughts a reality

At the moment you can get a FREE download of: "7 Easy Ways To Make Big Money While You Sleep!" But hurry up, the book will not be there forever!

Visit the web address below to receive your free eBook. I will also send a special heads-up Free books, Video Courses and other discounted resources to help you achieve your goals.

http://7waystomakemoneywhileyousleep.gr8.com/

Made in the USA
Lexington, KY
23 June 2016